COLLECTED POEMS

Also by Robert Nye

POETRY

Juvenilia 1, *Scorpion Press*, 1961
Juvenilia 2, *Scorpion Press*, 1963
Darker Ends, *Calder & Boyars*, 1969
Divisions on a Ground, *Carcanet Press*, 1976
A Collection of Poems 1955–1988, *Hamish Hamilton*, 1989

FICTION

Doubtfire, *Calder & Boyars*, 1967
Tales I Told My Mother, *Calder & Boyars*, 1969
Falstaff, *Hamish Hamilton*, 1976
Merlin, *Hamish Hamilton*, 1978
Faust, *Hamish Hamilton*, 1980
The Voyage of the Destiny, *Hamish Hamilton*, 1982
The Facts of Life and Other Fictions, *Hamish Hamilton*, 1983
The Memoirs of Lord Byron, *Hamish Hamilton*, 1989
The Life and Death of My Lord Gilles de Rais, *Hamish Hamilton*, 1990
Mrs Shakespeare: The Complete Works, *Sinclair-Stevenson*, 1993

EDITIONS

A Choice of Sir Walter Ralegh's Verse, *Faber*, 1972
William Barnes, Selected Poems, *Carcanet Press*, 1973
A Choice of Swinburne's Verse, *Faber*, 1973
The Faber Book of Sonnets, *Faber*, 1976
The English Sermon 1750–1850, *Carcanet Press*, 1976
A Selection of the Poems of Laura Riding, *Carcanet Press*, 1994

COLLECTED POEMS

Robert Nye

SINCLAIR-STEVENSON

This collection first published in Great Britain in 1995
by Sinclair-Stevenson
an imprint of Reed International Books Ltd
Michelin House, 81 Fulham Road, London SW3 6RB
and Auckland, Melbourne, Singapore and Toronto

A CIP catalogue record for this book
is available at the British Library

ISBN 1 85619 546 5

Typeset by Deltatype Ltd, Ellesmere Port, Cheshire
Printed and bound in Great Britain by
Mackays of Chatham PLC, Chatham, Kent

NOTE

The poems in this edition are collected from the following books and pamphlets:

Juvenilia 1 (Scorpion Press, 1961)
Juvenilia 2 (Scorpion Press, 1963)
Darker Ends (Calder & Boyars, and US: Hill & Wang, 1969)
Agnus Dei (Sceptre Press, 1973)
Five Dreams (Sceptre Press, 1974)
The Seven Deadly Sins: A Mask (Omphalos Press, 1974)
Divisions on a Ground (Carcanet Press, 1976)
A Collection of Poems 1955–1988 (Hamish Hamilton, 1989, and Sphere Books, 1991)
14 Poèmes (Editions Ottezec, 1994)
Henry James and Other Poems (US: R. L. Barth, 1995)

and from hitherto unpublished work.

Thanks are given to the publishers listed above for their kind permission to reprint poems first published by them, and to The Poetry/Rare Books Collection, University Libraries, State University of New York at Buffalo, for recovery of the texts of certain early poems here published for the first time.

CONTENTS

I

II

I

(1952–1957)

LISTENERS

Listening silence in the glass
The listening rain against.
All in the silent house asleep,
The rain and the glass awake;
All night they listen for a noise
No one is there to make.

All in the silent house asleep,
The rain and the glass awake;
Listening silence in the glass
The listening rain against.
All night they listen for a noise
Their silence cannot break.

KINGFISHER

At easter the kingfisher bird often
Stands on the snow's wrist all night long,
Unbubbling at morning the film of fire,
The big chrysalis of his green wings.

Hedgerow and clear meadow, frost-contoured,
Shift elegant in mist below the private hospital,
Between church and forest under him, prodigal
On pinnacles of sun, wanderer in new winds.

Kids with baked loaves in brown satchels
Skate down the polished lakes like spindrift fire.
My foam of light, my lambent spring-green watcher
Lonehovers above them, quick in the tight air.

Round waters thundergolden proud be prompt,
Cold punctual bird, Beloved signature.
As estuaries of flames boy's butter flesh,
My king bird eats the furtive easter fish.

MY MOTHER'S KITCHEN

The water butt
In our back yard
Has scum on it
As thick as lard.
I like to think
Caerleon on Usk
Burns bright here in
The summer dusk.
I stir the pot,
I stir it well—
Heaven has fallen
Into hell.
In the kitchen
My mother cooks
The legends of
Her cookery books.
Festering in
That pan pell-mell
My childhood has
A venial smell.

THAT RAVEN

That raven is mad
For it said, for it said:
A man in the morning
Will cut off your head.
To sew it back on again
Who has the art?
That woman behind you
Who's eating your heart.

A SONG OF SIXPENCE

My thumbs prick upon consequence.
Moths brush the wafers of grass
And the stickleback feels his thimble
Underwater house tremble
Where their warfare was.
In the black stream is sixpence.

Into my purse I put sixpence,
Nor bite my little finger at the words
Ants whisper round the chambers
Of a tussock of those strangers
Unwelcome to our tryst in the dark woods.
My thumbs prick upon consequence.

To pay whoever comes with no pretence
I have picked up this silver sixpence.
My thumbs prick upon consequence.

A TIME TO DANCE

Master, is it time to dance?
Look, sap is running down the lance
Where blood should be. The moon is red.
On such a night the living and the dead
Lie close together in the lap of chance.
Master, is it time to dance?

Master, is it time to dance?
Hark, all the bells from here to France
Are ringing in their towers. The sound
They make sends shivers through the ground
So that graves open at my glance.
Master, is it time to dance?

Master, is it time to dance?
In Luna's company I prance,
And ring the bells for her. The floor
Between my strides is level with the door.
My shadow tups me in my trance.
Dancer, it is time to dance.

MOON

The moon my madam coupled in Eden
In a bed of snow with the cripple Adam
And so do I lie with her larks without that garden.

HUNTSMEN

The fawn is oh but beautiful no friend of man
In summer then to catch her why do try
These many Robins clad in common green?
Tonight similarly in the netherlands
A blackbird whets his harmless ear with flutes.

With 'Horse and hattock, horse and away!' the oaf
Grins to beguile the unbeguiling rain
Cowardly on his instep, and skips out
To fall like rain the whole length of a street.

ALAN-A-DALE

No, not that fat friar who carried the sun
Across the stream on his back;
I am the henchman of moons, in green,
A stranger your dogs bark at.

I see people standing, seven miles away,
And I can hear them talk.
I sing, I say nothing, I dance as I walk
On May Day through the dusk.

Sweet briars and dog-roses, soft grails cupped with snow,
I bring in my fingers for one,
The eater of flowers, destroyer of men,
A woman as white as a thorn.

NOW

Night now lakes do like the darknesses
Of people and whose anger I expected.
Robin has engrossed his dead
In snow, at this harsh moment
Came Marian to the green wood first,
With dew a grey compare
And frost across her hair,
Rats running before
The lips in a laughter of foul bough-shadow.

They say she broke frogs
Much as I clench a creature now.
Mistress, did you pause
Even as I pause now, but fearing no vengeance?

BELLADONNA

The black glove fits your left white hand
With an appropriate black.
Your white glove on the other hand
Is freckled with blood.

A pied piper plays one tune:
Black and white are the same,
And left and right the ends of an egg
Under a blind hen.

Because you do not know my name
And never shall know me,
You lie in the stem of the mottled dark
To see what you can see.

Around us go my gloves, grey gloves—
They are empty as empty wind.
Your right hand is a ladybird,
Your left hand is a hand.

TO HIMSELF

Foreigner in foreign country
Not my countryman,
Stranger to strange company
No stranger,
Logical interloper
I think you are benighted
By your own grief
Of fitting in too well.

OTHERWISE ELSEWHERE

You slept, and listened as the rain fell
To an unpetitioning herald
Awakening the servants of elsewhere.
Otherwise I was there.

Otherwise and elsewhere
We were Lord and Lady Landless,
Our arms liable to trill with blood
If on each other's names we called.

Perhaps I dream I dream now
I dream I sleep, as rain falls,
To think you otherwise,
Myself elsewhere.

COBWEB

For who shall be of cobweb
And who himself?
A shallow wheel, no deeper
Than cobweb, keeps us.

This weft dishevelled habit
Forgotten by the weaver
Will it keep us together
When you are of your cobweb
And I myself?

THE CHERRY TREE

His answer to the cherry tree
She peoples with lack-lustre fruit:
'This was a pretext of the night,
The nightingale's unlucky perch
For renaissance of his pain,
A darker index of the moon,
The radicle from foot to star
Both feet go searching for.'

Such common prayers are by day
His question in the cherry tree,
An ever-during commonplace
Of 'you' and 'us' and 'them' and 'me'.
She bids the dusky blossoms haste
Her butterfly into a moth,
To wash the cherries from his wings
And dry his wings along dry bark.

A MOTH

'See, there, her face behind us, on the pane
That runs with night. She watches jealously
While I undress your shadow on the ceiling.
She comes and goes between us if we nap
Too near the grate, or walk before this lamp,
Sleep-walkers leading the blind colts of sleep
For them to fill the steps we make for them.'

'Put out the light. There is no one behind us—
Only a moth who wants to die too soon.
Or let her in, and welcome, for she'll find
Fire's not so hot nor flame so flattering when
You have no choice but burning, and that's hard.
Now, sleep, and no more dreams. I'll leave my best
Shoes, heels under, to ride away nightmare.'

SAYING GRACE

Wherehowsoever he may say please
That pleasant lover on his knees
Rises no thank-you lover from
His dear's unholy martyrdom
Until he has the manners when-
ever she prays to say 'Amen,
Amen, God be it so
And glory be and to God go
The godliness, if the chastity
God gave her she will give to me
That I can be as chaste again
As when I did not know her, Amen.'

My grandmother has taught me well
The way to pray to heaven or hell:
To be all things to all men
But only one thing to one woman,
To drink to her and to behave
Not with the favour of a slave
But absurd gentlemanliness
So be it to that or this
Or the other if I am able
To wait on her at the Lord's table,
Attend her talk of him and after
Say grace that is my talk of her.

With hand on heart and hat in hand
I say my prayers at your command
And give thanks for today:
This morning when we said good-day,
This evening when we said good-bye,
And the night that went by.

Yet if I loved you here and now
In little language, thee and thou,
With no disgrace like yesterday
And without any prayers to pray
Or knees to kneel on, I would love
You more than christendom knows of.

I will love you, my only one,
Begging no pardon, granting none.
I shall not stop to say a grace
Before I kiss your breakfast face.
I must love you with a hard heart
And make you love me, for your part,
With few soft words but many a grunt
As I speak volumes in your cunt.
Tomorrow, when pigs play pianners,
May such distemper mar my manners
So that at least as good as true
I am as graceless, dear, as you.

SHADOWLESS

There was no shadow there
Where your feet were.
We did not blemish
Each other when we went
Invisibly together
In dewless pantomime.

For me to be transparent
You took me for your own.
So the burlesque went on:
My leg ashamed your step,
My heart assumed your beat,
I had you confident.

But I was too much yours
And you went with yourself
To other beds, to be
Their shadow, because mine
Followed your heel too well,
Too well for constancy.

Wherever you are now,
Whoever follows you,
I would tell him of you:
To love a thing of nothing
I have been nobody,
And you must love her so

For she is shadowless
In the evening's brightness.
O shadowless is she
And you must love her so—
Seek not to be her shadow for
When night comes, shadows go.

OTHER TIMES

Midsummer's liquid evenings linger even
And melt the wind in autumn, when bonfires
Burn books and bones, and lend us foreign faces.
At such a heart's November I might wish
There was some way back through the calendar
Again to find you and to lose your love.

I might—but there's no eager winter weather
To my remembering. Our appetites
Were satisfied with spring, and cloyed by June.
If August brought us famine . . . Well, no matter.
It serves us right that when I'd think of you
My memory comes hankering back to autumn.

The gloam rains slowly; fireworks kick with green,
Attach all marigoldal to the hand.
A weasel dancing by the sallows calls
Windsor to mind, and when you went tip-toe
By the breathing statue of the Copper Horse
For bashful fear it would come down to us.

The roundabouts and swings wear canvas shrouds
In gardens our ghosts visit. A bat walks—
Hare-lip, shrill membrane, hooks—as it were you.
A bat's newfangled walk, as it were you.
Dear flackering bat, or ghost, my faithless head
Has not forgot you, though our haunts are gone.

And you have gone, though your autumnity
Remains to vex me in each hip and haw
Which early frosts have ripened to perfection.
'Do not remember me for I am here
At other times,' you said. At other times
I can remember but have loved enough.

REMEMBERING NO NAME

Remembering no name I would remember
No name of my mother, my grandmother,
Nor nickname before I knew her, knowing
Solace in loss no more to seal
The surly latchet of a tear, no more
Unknown would I dare remember
Salt, shell and ladle indelibly
Blessing the bitter font of me
With her sweet titles, now or never
Giving what she has given back
For to name the faces I remember.
But no name I know is the name of my mother
Nor of that dear anonymous other
Who knew a man, nor my nickname,
But the name of the face of a child, a child
Who has no childhood to remember.

SEASONING

Kids of the hatter weighting down low larch—
Their nimble skins hang fire to suit each icicle.
Fruit is coatmakers in March.

Butterflies in your fingernail,
Maidenhair round the water-pail.
Hips, haws, and berries that parch.

Four ways to spoil the woods with evening;
Four quarters of the reasons
For a rape of the seasons

In onanistic spleen.
Four tellers of we-told-you-so
Telling what might have been.

INCANTATION

O spurred black cockerel
Yet clawed spectacular
On crusted frost, on moon of cedarwood.

O harvest white apples,
Thick small seed with honey,
Red cider and chunked butter.

O glacier craftsmen,
Sprawled robbers on a mountain,
Loot flesh, gold sores of the fever of thieves.

O unseal seawrack
And trivial veins break,
Letting, in low shells, tears thrice-simple.

O lips on seas feast
Thy knobbled raindrops.
My teeth touch, bite the narrow God-root.

TO MARY VIRGIN

Lament thy charities, O Queen Mary,
And lily mercies nor a throne afford.
Be each in each and both itself because
Thy grace is prayer's simplicity.

Our Lady also we implore
By lovingkindness, by still waters,
By the whistling stirrup of the sea-horse,
In Broceliande no injury befall us.

To pray thy silence is to covet Hell
For cloven snow more silence could not tell
Chaste a reality that dreams the world
So everlasting and so small.

Memory of blood, we play with willow hoops.
O Lady among handmaidens
The rainbow's ghost is on thy fingers
Watching the sun caught captive jest to tears.

O host of sleep be Sleep and, for us,
Love undiscovered lost not to be found.

THE LAST SUPPER

We have not knelt down at this table
To also gorge with the rabble
Of Giant Treacle,
Who when blood falls on Haymarket
Washes both his hands in it.
Our treason is high treason,
A crown cast in the beans.
His house this is but whose household?
Kitchens are upset underfoot
And toads and frogs from saucepans hover
To mushrooms, flap! their crackled backs
Go under the cooks' thumbs.
Queer things are happening,
Who calls for vermin?
His red curls fill our plate.

The tailor hid his tail behind
His whiskers, tucked it like a scarf,
And 'This is my well-beloved,' said the cat
Scratching our sleeve, 'hark.'
But the visitor sat
Down with never a word
Uncrossing his knife and fork.
After the wine no usual talk
As darkness staled on the windowpane
Corrected the thought that here was a king
Come to an angry reckoning.
We are enamoured of the dead
In this fair land . . . A game of cards . . . ?
'I love a true soldier best,' he said,
Picking the bits from his teeth.

The scaffold is a nuptial couch
In Lyonnesse, in Lyonnesse.
Fellows are magisterial
And there's no neutral evil
In bird or beast.
But here the dew that crimes the grass
Laces our slippers as we pass
With sacrosanct apostasy,
'Go!' screams the lark and 'Come with me!'
The badger orders, fumbling
Into a fresh grave.
Our trespasses are just as frost
Purging the Giant's sharp fingers to excuse
Another way of love . . .
Shut up, you fools!

As it was he looked comfortable enough
For ale and walnuts
And crisp toast lapped with butter,
Instead dull pistol drew and shot
The paint into the block.
When I went riding
I met Robin
With the fawn of sudden seeming
In his real hood, in the pool:
Which is the cross and which the man?
To be at one is difficult
Within the margin of three nails
As hair grows on the head.
By open bread may you understand
I had not love enough to rage.

We heard the jolting ant beneath the trestle
Be lief with his cautels,
He murders no sods who are sober.
The Giant's hands

Composed the garden
Cooling the furious petals,
The settled carpets shut with nard.
The hill lay in the hill below the hill.
Be absolute, eagle, to the child
You take for lust
By the altering moon
Over impossible and flashing stones
To this restaurant.
Well, thank-you thank-you, we are all
Safe in our towers that will not fall.

THE HOLY EXPERIMENT

Byron beside Augusta found
Nothing about her shrewd behind
He had not known, or guessed, before.

She was no manicon,
Sweet-singing Edleston,
Sob-sister that sort,

Nor handy courtesan
Cold as a whetstone,
With soap for a backbone—

Nothing like that.
She was a cat
Without cradle for kittens,

Without nine lives or tails
(One life and one tail
He told without fail),

Without bell, without mittens,
A lady cat-bugger—
O glory Augusta.

Byron said 'Figs!
It rains cats and dogs,
My love is natural.'

It rains cats and dogs.
But do dogs miaow
Or cats go bow-wow?

No, Byron, no.
No, no, Augusta.
Cockchafer, no cockloft.

SAINT JOAN

A thing in the form of a woman
By name of the Pucelle
Was burned by the soldiers at Rouen
After a proper trial.
She was a relapsed heretic
And excommunicate catholic,
Apostate, idolatress,
Divineress and sorceress;
A devil from Lorraine
Whence devils come
In the dress of women
As everyone knows.

THE LADIES' TREE

Amen, amen the Ladies' Tree falls in me:
May in my arm-pits, beech-nuts in my grasp
Bristling the down on my legs at loggerheads
With honeybine distraught about the hem,
No lily lentlier, and in my custody
Ramage and nestling, all the wayward tree
More lovely than its leaves my eyes and eyelids.

The wind of it back-wounded with the fall
I am, and not the tree nor its likeness
Nor mother of so pollardly a giant.
The lichen Ladies at my whisper all
Out of breath into these branches come
For an enleafment of my glimpse of them
In bark so lickerish and smally cold.

Motherly are the pipits on the bough
And pipit feathers in the thorny well;
'Saw down the old woman' is all their song
And would be my song in the Ladies' Tree.
If I am not in the grace of God
God take me there, and so may he keep me
If I am in his grace all unawares.

THE VOICES

Amen, amen a citadel falls in me
Sealed in white scrolls of armour
For now the siege of angels burns my flesh.

See, see they sing these painful colours,
These tender rivers in my hand's division.
All France is but a vein across my breasts.

Such spin and spin the tiny oceans,
My whirlpool eardrum, snowball navel,
Saint Catherine's kisses like my threads of blood.

Orleans, Orleans in regions of great rivers
Struts now the greatest River:
A bridge athwart the thoroughfare of God.

BEYOND ENDEARMENTS

Beyond endearments then I come to you,
My dear, and promise to be false
As luck will let me because I love you.
Slut! to be Queen of this and to be this
In your queenliness, how can I love you?
How can I love you still knowing your love
Is the hell-fire that burns all but your heart?
It is because your familiars
Love me, and they will keep me from the fire.
O Salamander when I saw you burn
Your burning burnt more than I saw or am;
For you I loved because you were not you
And thus it was I did not speak to you
And tell my love. We were not beautiful
Nor in one ugly spirit popular,
Nor altogether nearer death together,
Nor private either. Yet I loved you—
What else, what else, what else was I to do?

II

(1958–1962)

DEDICATIONS

Begrudged by the promising pencraft of my name—
On the flyleaves of books I thought were mine—
Dedicating each poem to you as if
It hoped its nine letters would be read
Into the classic authorship, and free-hearted
Of Love-until-our-names-are-both-forgotten
(In such shorthands as half-admired their remembrance)
I could not yet refuse to sign myself
Or much regret you and your books are mine
For I loved the girl who read them for her virtue
And now you have my vices and my name.

NIGHT WATCH

Watching for my son to fall asleep, I fell asleep first
And woke in a dream to watch him sleep in this world
(of all probable worlds worst)
Where he must wake in nightmare, not born free,
And nod with one eye open, on me.

Not that I would love him for heaven's sake or, worse,
Make him immortal with a curse.
Dreaming he slept I kept him safe from harm
Who was keeping me awake, and my heart warm.

Lullabies, my jackanapes, are out of date
But to remember them it is not too late:
Sing hushabye then, however much music it take,
However I wake watching for my son to wake.

THE STOAT

As I walked home a stoat ran round
About me with a womanish sound
Dancing neither high nor low
On an oblique and wily toe,
Eyes like blue cinders in the snow.

Those eyes so used to rat and hare
Fixed mine in a moon-blinded stare
Until I saw you everywhere:
Your dress that drift of smothering snow,
Your face her face, your step her slow
And rampant dancing, in and out,
And up and down and round about,
Until I felt the hot flesh stir
Between my legs, but not for her,
Nor yet for you, and standing still
On whited ground, against my will,
I felt my heart leap to my throat
And cry out for the dancing stoat.

SIGNS

Perch at play in a water-hole
Can be spellbound by a telegraph-pole,
Cockle the wires up in their spines.
Perhaps you have dismissed such signs
With an angry kiss?
Other signs you may not dismiss:
The salmon speared by torchlight, or this
Death-rattle rising from your throat
In dimming air to see a snow-white stoat.

THE HERON

The moon is in her shroud. A heron
Like a sickle dipped in feathers, knee-
deep among streaming stars, a taciturn
And wistful fisher, starves out of her trance
And combs into thin air stiffly askance.

The moon is rising. O heron, heron
Where is there more to drown in than the sea?

AT THE WHITE CITY

Count all the numerals rotting round the hem
Of the red gown you wore at races
When none of your dogs won, or came in second.

Numbers and colours equally confuse you.
The hare runs true to form, but cannot please you
Who bark in discontinuous antitheses.

Will you not have the Bibles burned? or writ
In a green Tote upon the bursting earth
Where you will lie, not dead, but not in love?

Behind the stadium a gutter's cheeks
Blush at drowned tipsters, their alchemical hats,
And blanch again with shivering betting-slips.

Will you not cry: *If I confined myself to error*
I could be true as any liar
More truthfully confined to error? You will lose
Each way, in promiscuous either-or.

HER NAMES

Her names are birds, who wantonly
Shakes the wet fledgelings from the nest
And gives her hand where they would cling
Bewildered, soft, and limp of wing
  To have me as her guest.

'A peacock in Leucadia
  Loved me before you came.
And yet for all his peacock-pride
He died the eager day I died
  And never knew my name.
  And would you be the same?'

I would not be the same, my dove.
I'd name you plain, if I could learn
To leave the winding falcon or
To know a hawk from a handsaw,
  A handsaw from a hern.

REVENANT

If through that mirror's crack in not quite dusk
You see, or remember, the only ghost you know
Beyond your own ghost on the frost-worked pane—
Under a map of the Land of Cockaigne
A child asleep on his arms at a high desk,
Dreaming of puppets, poems, and sherbet powder—
Why not elect to love him, for he was
A boy who never learned to tell the time
And you're late coming home.

THE BROKEN SEA

His heart (swollen or wasted with sea-music) cries:
'The waves are heart-beats on the shore.
How slow they come! A broken heart dies slowly.
The Sea is not in love with me, or is she?
The Sea has not forsaken me, or has she?
How cold she is! And yet I love her wholly.'
So more or less and mostly more
His heart (swollen or wasted with sea-music) dies.

HERE AND THERE

Here and there, by and by,
Some of us like to die
Without dishonour, gravely.

Our ghostly comforter
Comes and goes, ghostlier
Than you who discomfit her.

If I say 'dead' to you,
Dreamless in bed with you,
Can true death or love be true?

And if I dream you near?
I would not love you, dear,
If we died there, and not here.

UNLIKENESS

Exile of skin unlikely similar
She likes unlikeness, Our Lady's shroud.
Our Lady she dislikes, her sigh too loud
A wilderness of the familiar.

RALEGH SAID

Ralegh said on the night-watch
Our Thames is richer in its seam
Than any rainbow round a waterspout.
The whale's straked country
Floods all that sky under grinders.
Other absence, other inconsequence:
Sloops melting with sail copy
The sheer horizon, blue mists itself
On blue until we dream
Darkness falls like a dead brightness
And the sea's full of heaven (or Gravesend).
But do not use the wind but master it
With words the waves write on the sand:
Names for the night. Learn them, said Ralegh.

CHRISTMAS EVE

On Christmas Eve in ivory air
I drag the old moon by the hair
And trot her through the cobbled snow.

The dark is bright as Calvary.
The naked stars across the black
Web of the night crawl spiderly.

Child, sleep while you can. Tomorrow
I will tell you another story.
Now ride in your dreams the mare Glory,
The stud Death, and the wild colt Sorrow.

FAMILIAR TERMS

You say I love you for your lies?
  But that's not true.
I love your absent-hearted eyes—
  And so do you.

You say you love me for my truth?
  But that's a lie.
You love my tongue because it's smooth—
  And so do I.

You say they love who lie this way?
  I don't agree.
They lie in love and waste away—
  And so do we.

AGAINST THE QUEEN

Against the Queen the Queen's men
Come into their own again,
From cavalier in other beds
Become roundheads.
Fond of the white disease
Themselves they bleed, because
Their war is civil with it,
As ours is private.

Crowned heart, my keeper
Out of all misfortune
Deep upon deeper,
Keep me, keep her,
Lest at our coronation
Your rebel dreams make
Plots of such treason
That not for my sake
You cry yourself awake.

THE CANDLES

They watch the candles melt together
In little deaths, slow inch by inch,
Two mortal enemies in love.

'What do you do?'
                    'I wonder whether
Their vehemence can last the night.
Perhaps some long-lost tenderness will keep
Their lust alive? Or must they waste and wither?'

Two mortal enemies in love
With death, and burning for each other,
They watch the weeping candles melt together.

SHADOWS

Seek not to be her shadow for
When night comes shadows go
Into the darkness following
Her footfalls to and fro,
Bewildered by her wandering
In the bewildering snow.

Do you suppose your silences
Will warm her shadowy heart?
Or that by lying at her feet
You'll learn her truthful art?
You might as well adore the moon
Where shadows end, and start.

SELF-CURSE

Bitter, be bitterer;
Rue, be more rueful;
Ghosts go through you
And not you them.

When you are gone
May no man mourn;
Nor woman grieve
By your green grave;
Let none recall
You were at all.

Bitter, be bitterer;
Rue, be more rueful;
Ghosts go through you
And not you them.

IN PARENTHESIS

(This is not a poem I will give to you
To read, my dear, my reader, but not my dear reader.
I do not want you to read it in your heart.
I do not want you to think this is a secret
Between you and me, not even a secret
Between me and me, as in my dream of it.
I do not want to write this and I did not
Remember, although I know I shall; not even because
Of the chance that it may not lie, for certainly
This will exorcise nothing. But a little
It has been with me since and I must satisfy the heart's content
As your heart will disbelieve or, rather, misunderstand.
For if you thought I loved you
That would be better; better ever, I mean, than this—
Than the truth you'll not believe.)

COMPLINE

Born into a world already dead
The funeral bores us with its brilliant doom;
Yet being jealous not to let our shadows
Fall in the grave, we kneel as is seemly
And do not grin too much behind clasped hands.
We pray the resurrection, when it comes,
Will not prove irresistible.

LET IT GO

Snow fell so quick
That snow was melt
Before it lasted on the ground.
The fleering pane
Of gloomy fire
Turned steadfastness to water also.

CIGARETTE SMOKE

A hooping in the firs,
A looming on the weir—
The wind and the rain are also lost.
I pull my collar close.
I light a cigarette.
And how can I forget
Your unfamiliar ghost
If in the glimmer here
The smoke is exorcised, and disappears?

THE FURIES

To spite the Furies
Some poets blow
Half their brains out.
How furiously
Those half-wits then
Fool with their verses
To please the Furies.

DEAR EXORCIST

I came to grief from dry dismay
With truthful tears, dear exorcist,
Tears kissing on my sorry sheaf
Of poetry and platitude.
You were the spendthrift and the thief
Of tristful sleep and trustful day
And the black night's similitude.

My crooked heart you could not break
And left me thus disconsolate
At our broken beatitude;
I came to grief importunate
To know our dissimilitude.
Let us be true, for untruth's sake!
My semblances assimilate
To your dissembling desuetude,
Dear exorcist, and make believe
I lie because I lie awake.

THE FOX

The hunt is hunting
In the black forest.
Lost horns call night.
The hunt is hunted.

Dark Helen, the fox
Is your paramour.
Your innocence
Is lewd of pity.
Gabriel and his hounds
Lust nakedly after
Forsaken passions.

Bright Sparta, the fox
Is your enemy.
Your innocence
Is a memory of guilt.
Darkly, of your demons?
Or of your beauty, brightly?

OWL

'Howlet,' she whispers, 'howlet, owlet, owl,'
Kissing the owl-light on the windowpane
Before her breath can shrink from it, a warm fleck
In freckled glass.
                    'Love!' And he burns his lips
With what no words or kisses plainly speak of—
Laughing to greet his cold reflection coldly.

HUMPTY DUMPTY

Higher mathematics led him to
Decimal Folly where
He broke his head on a vulgar fraction
Out of love with calculus;
Differential heaven addled to infinity
In the broken halves of his brain
As he waxed qualitatively bald.

'O Rose,' he cried to a rather square root,
'O Time,' to an integer;
'O Christ, O Christ,' to a crucified surd,
'Sweet Truth,' to algebra.
Thus and thus he baptised a logarithm
In philosophical haste
Lest it should multiply.

Zero came after death.
Before he could pull on his wig
The sacred serials blessed him,
Aliquot antilogarithms lay
Like dandruff all around:
God in great numbers was divided
And added him together.

THE VIXEN

A vixen from that turbary lost the hunt
At a five-barred gate with a six-barred shadow.
Rowan shed a windless livery; a crown,
Dew-dull, dripped on a damasked rose-bush; the turf
Glued the vixen's scream and a scream of horses.

Slimy cobweb still bellies, unjettisoned,
In the cracked gate-hinge; but the king spider starves.
My father munches flies, hamstrings the hunters.
My heir, the blind prince, duels in the cathedral.
Vixen, where is the earth, the earth will hide me?
Vixen, where is your earth? Your earth will hide me.

CIRCE TO ULYSSES

Stand on the North Wind, atheist,
And dream of beaches where kings dive for stars.
Listen to high water in shells, or spars
Clinking up shingle. Nor moly nor bees-wax
Can make you deaf to your own voice
Who have seen Atlantis,
Its less than grace, and the unfortunate isles;
Whose moon-hauled keel remembers stark gold miles
Over that pack ice where rainbows kiss,
Drumming deep defiles.

My starlight cargo poisoned you too soon.
There is no antidote against the moon.

A SONG OF LOGIC

When she was conch and quill gathering in the outsands
Those ruffians made her nose bleed with a slate.
She blasphemed the extinct gods, sipped
Her lipstick sleepily, and sang a song of logic.

Neither were her wounds wholly incestuous.
The blue blood (her melted and bewildered rage)
Deflowered those ruffians with absurd anguish.
They sang the song of logic learned from her.

Kinsmen, criminals, and wiseacres, the jury
Of pangs has found you guilty of philosophy.
Your sentence: Innocence for Life. (With good conduct
To be commuted perhaps to crucifixion.)

Have the prisoners nothing to say? Something to sing:
A song of logic sung by the plaintiff.
Or are we yet responsible for her dreams
That they should teach us such a rude tenderness?

Waking, she hesitates to dip again
Into the dim pool closing on her pillow.
Should she hasten out heel-first over the quicksands
Might not the footprints she smutched be her own?

COUNTER-CLOCKWISE

Clocks in this house that we stop to listen to
Stop—hearing whose last words? Gnomon-shadow stabs
At our shadow on the sundial's other words.
A gleam in the hour-glass (how did we suck out
Our shadow?) quickly scrambles against the thread
In the prim neck: to be buried under sand.
For us, death by hanging on a pendulum.

Tick (clocks have clean hands that never point at us)
Tock (clocks have faces that never blanch or blush)
The clicking clock wastes time, and so do we.
On the back stair have we not nodded to
The black man with the keys? Can we not hear
The softly bleeding tell-tale slow *tick-tock*
Under the floorboards? It is not our hideous heart.

The heart breaks counter-clockwise—let it break!
Love is eternity half-killing time
From chime to chime, from kiss to kiss to kiss,
From death to death, from heaven and hell to this.
Once we might have stopped to listen, but now
It is too late for listening clocks to stop.
In a minute all the hours will strike together.

WHITE AIR

White air half dews and sallows
You lit there at All Hallows.
In the whirlwind of white air
You rode the wild Night Mare
Till she was meek and mild
As any christened child.
Beldame, I loved you then
More than those hallowed men,
And love you now again
The air is white with sallows
Between us and All Hallows.

THE LARK

The lark from his nest in a hoofprint springs
Up, up, up, up, trilling dew from his wings,
And busily rests, and sings, and sings.
I watch and listen, wondering why
His song's sad sweetness, a laughing sigh,
Reminds me only that I must die.

CAROLS

As I hook up my jacket the arms are stolen
And cut off from behind.
On your bed my shadow lies
And bleeds, nor may you stem it with a kiss.
Breath in the lamp. Remember the waits,
Latin for Easter, and a child whispering 'makeless'
Up the glamouring staircase
(My sleeve blooded,
A dagger in a sampler)
And who replies 'O my agroted heart',
Disposing in sleep:
'When you have built a city, husband, burn it.'
Ghosts in the lamp. Another cries 'makeless'
And none replies. The carollers are gone.

GULLIVER'S PROGRESS

Death said: 'Husband, what does this coldness mean?
Why have you gone away from me with the Dean?'
'Alas,' answered Gulliver, 'giants and dwarfs can
Couple, but are no companions for a gentleman.'

BEACHCOMBERS

Flood-tide rising ebb-tide falling
Drowned the Queen in the bell;
Her heart lolled on the clapper
A toll or two, then fell
Down where her mind had fallen
Ringing a high-pitched knell.

Columbus locked in his cabin,
Drunk on Atlantic dew,
Dreamt of the crucifixion.
Riding at anchor, his crew
Lusted after blue dolphins,
Whispered: 'The Wandering Jew!'

No angelus no America
Have we to undiscover,
Who both have been beachcombers
Where the lost sea has no lover.
O Sea, run deep below me
As you are high above her.

A GOLDEN KNOT

In the small hours of the needful night
I watch you comb your rainy hair
And braid it up in a golden knot.

The tortoiseshell in the ember-gleam
Like glazed frost on a silver thaw
Trickles bleak with its own dewiness.

The bed—narrow, cold; a bleb of blood
On the pillow. Your powder pots
And puffs snow-pollen the black mirror.

You are my memory and my heart.
But is this love: the needless need
To hang myself in a golden knot?

AT LAST

Dear, if one day you hear my heart,
Under your cheek, forget to start
Its life-long argument with my head,
Do not rejoice that I am dead
And need some graver sort of bed,
But say: 'At last he's found the art
To hold his tongue and lose his heart.'

A DIVINE COMEDY

Sober Orpheus' singing head
Sang of Beatrice as it bled,
Despite the ruthless moon.
O holy, holy Lethe.

Dante of the foxskin cap
Lay in Eurydice's lap,
Sour milk asleep in honey.
O Lethe, holy Lethe.

It was Homer's holy writ
Took that head and buried it
In a divine comedy.
O holy, holy, holy Lethe.

THE GRASSHOPPER

Patience wears out stones: and poets too
Are worn out by a patience
For poetry, and for the unquiet poem.
But is the grasshopper impatient when
She drowns in autumn dew, a meagre fury?

THE LOOKING-GLASS

We have no mirrors in this house because
There are no faces here for mirroring
But broken lineaments staring and glaring
From table-top and spoons, whose haunted kind—
Features and creatures and illumination—
Is the self-spectacle or pageant of
Illusion, and a prospect of the Devil.

O glass, O glass, O lying looking-glass,
Your strangeness has not changed, as I have changed,
Despite this candle's shroud of crooked wax
And the cold sweat in the cricket's cry.
I am the last of a discrete lineage
Who raised the dead by looking at themselves.
But who are you behind me and before?

All my delusions are no more than lies;
I live in undeceived bewilderment.
If I do not doubt your absurdity,
Is this absurd? Because there are no mirrors
Fit to kiss you, must I not? I loathed you
Because you looked like me. Have I changed much?
Of course I love you, or love you of course.

WIDEAWAKE WATER

Washing sleep away in a bowl of warm rain,
Or with fistfuls of snow, or a melted moon,
Have you never wondered whether your dreams
In the jealous bed are not worth the dreaming?
Whether your whispers to death in the dark
Are less than the gossip of wideawake water?

Others there are who will greet you more gently
And kiss you less softly than wideawake water,
Less honest than water, in love with your dreams.
But I shall not love you for what you imagine,
For more than you dream, or less than you hope,
Washing sleep away in a bowl of warm rain.

NO SECOND SIGHT

You see, I have no gift of second sight
To look into your eyes and watch my heart,
Nor any truthfulness, but untrue love
Feeding the fire I am a shadow of.
The night is long enough. We have all night.
Only blind lovers love at the first sight.

III

(1963–1969)

DARKER ENDS

Here's my hand turned to shadows on the wall—
Black horse, black talking fox, black crocodile—
Quick fingers beckoning darkness from white flame,
Until my son screams, 'No! chase them away!'

Why do I scare him? Fearful of my love
I'm cruelly comforted by his warm fear,
Seeing the night made perfect on the wall
In my handwriting, if illegible,
Still full of personal beasts, and terrible.

Abjure that art—it is no true delight
To lie and turn the dark to darker ends
Because my heart's dissatisfied and cold.
To tell the truth, when he is safe asleep,
I shut my eyes and let the darkness in.

A BAT IN A BOX

The long cold cracked and I walked in the cracks
To pay the rent for the first time in weeks
And pick our post up from the farm on the top road.

That done— 'Has your son,' said the farmer's wife,
'Ever seen a bat in a box? I have one
You could take back to show him.'

And I imagined how a bat in a box
Would beat its bloodshot wings, and comb itself
With greedy claws, and eat up flies and beetles;

And how, when hanging by the wing-hooks, it
Would sleep, long ears tucked under, as if cloaked:
And how its tameness might in fact confound me.

I did not take it, back down through the snow
To show my son.
                    Why did I not do so?

To tell you, I would have to undo winter,
Thaw my bare spirit, waste its bitterness,
Losing the wry frost with some deeper drifts.

A bat,
        in a box.
                Just think of it.

THE SAME SONG

You dream a song and I begin to sing it
In a false voice, and so the song is ruined
That was word-perfect in your head. In anger,
You tell me to be silent. 'Still, how strange
That you should sing the same strange song I'm dreaming.
Perhaps I hummed or drummed it? and you heard.'

No, music, I've no natural explanations.
You did not sing—but I have mocked your song
In broken accents, for my own amusement.
One day with a true voice I'd like to tell
How sometimes we catch breath and sing together
The same strange song, knowing we need no other.

A LOAF OF BREAD

I went to the road for food, and found
Common surprise in a loaf of bread,
Holding my breath with the breath of it
And knowing that when I breathed again
It would indeed be morning and a loaf of bread
Clean in the carton there with other
Necessary purchases
Of a son unprodigalled, trying to play father.
I had not thought I could be so astonished.

Bread! I sat under the hedge
Out of a hungry wind, and the just-baked loaf
Was matter of fact as I sank my teeth
Into its crust and nibbled, then took
Swift bites out of its good and risen wholeness.

If I'd remembered I'd have sung for joy
Just to myself and the loaf in the commonplace morning—
Joy at dismissing for ever, or the time being,
Guilt at the boy I was for standing
Outside shop windows, sly nose squashed flat
Against the pane, dreaming on galleons and castles
Of cream and pastry, marshmallow, doughnut, shortbread,
Until I thought I'd faint for want of those
Unnecessary sweets which were all I wanted.

I didn't remember till now, and now's too late.
'The birds have been eating the bread again,' you say,
Cutting the bad part out.
Thus satisfied—
With bread and the perfect alibi—how could I sing?

A WINTER SURPRISE

Lost is the night, and loose
The day's astonishment.
I cannot bring you back
The summer way we went.
I cannot love you now
As once I loved myself,
With such a rare wild unforgiving heart.

And yet I love you with
Most gifts the evening has,
Touching your hair, your lips
With a winter surprise—
So that you speak of pain,
The child quick in your womb,
And wish the day undone, the night unknown.

AN EXCELLENT MATCH

I am your glass, and mirror everywhere
The fires you burn to see, or fear to be;
The man you wish you were, I am for you,
Reflecting who you are in what we do;
Yet I am yours too much, too perfectly—

For look, our likeness has an end, and there
Beyond the glass, deeper than your self-looking,
I rage, in blank suspicion, and half-mocking,
Completed by the knowledge I can share
Those images you give me, your reflections,
Though these shine otherwise, in false directions.

It makes no difference even when the glass
Grows dark with more than night, or streaked with day
Larger than likely. Radiance and stain
Fall on you in a cold familiar way,
Fixed in a constancy I cannot pass.
The colour black is busy here, that's plain.

ANNIVERSARY

This is the wooden wedding—
Five years marred or married.
You came of your strength,
I went of my weakness,
To a time where one said, 'I love you'—
Meaning, 'I am lost. Find me!'—
And the other could not sleep in an empty bed.

Now we sleep too well together
And our separate hearts dream variously.
Such self-caressing dreams . . .
You have learned my weakness, and it suits you.
I have wasted your strength, and it chokes me.
And yet you speak of this
As an anniversary. And so it is.

We will celebrate our wooden wedding
With poems written by sentimental liars
Who found love easy, a comfortable sun
To shiver under in chill complaisance,
And not as it is—the difficult moon
Crying 'Adore me! Adore me!' and then turning
Her naked back on mortal adoration
To go whoring after other moons, other devourers.

It is an occasion for happiness
And we are happy in our perfect ruin,
Being wooden both and hacking at each other
In the name of truth, though it be only fretwork.
Five years marred or married—
Time enough for regret perhaps
In the next five, in the happier returns,
When the heart has turned to tin.

GONE OUT

Whenever you leave the house I write a poem—
To answer you or bring your questions home?
When you are here my words belong to you,
You take my breath, not as you used to do,
But for sufficient purposes of speech.
You hang upon my language like a leech.

Yet when you've gone an hour the poem fades
And I have little left but blots and shades
Of meaning, and I mean all that I say,
Which draws me out to stand and watch the way
Through the dim valley, hoping you'll come back
To give my words the simpleness they lack.

GATHERING STICKS

Snow in the wind and pine-smoke blown back
Down the awkwardly patched-up chimney-stack
On her house that's at home by the wood.
Gathering sticks in the frosty dell
I stop to watch that smoke, I know well,
Which has come from the fire of her mood.

Sticks will be chopped and new water drawn
From the spring in the side of a winter dawn
By others, that's understood,
But will they turn back with cleaner hearts
Through snow and wind to where the smoke starts,
And with better fire in their blood?
Perhaps they'll just turn, as I turn now,
Not knowing why, not caring how,
With a love that does no one much good.

AN ABSENCE OF NETTLES

I like nettles, but I took
An old scythe for your sake
To clean the way where you would walk
And make it possible
For your foreshadowed flowers.

An evening I worked there,
And another, longer; gripping
The ancient handles with a clumsy craft,
Swinging the rusty blade about my knees,
Crouched to listen to it.

The keen heads of nettles
Lopped without pity
Were raked and carried up
To a black-hearted bonfire;
The shaven earth was ready.

I plucked out such roots
As the hands can find,
And cast away pebbles;
Weeding and watering
My own grave.

But now—no flowers have come
To fit your shadows;
The earth will not accept
The seeds you sow. And who can care for
An absence of nettles, an ungrowing place?

A MIDNIGHT CREATURE

In the sea's false cradle
Most desolately rocked
Or on the baffling edge of sleep
Where dreams fall fast,
There have I seen the daemon
And known him with my heart
Who had been otherwise unknown,
A midnight creature, half unloved,
No more to me than you.

A TROUT

Waiting for you, I sat and watched a trout
And found some warp of comfort in the thought
That I might catch or counterfeit his style
Of silence, to and fro, a subtle fool
In the dark places of the yielding stream,
But in that deeper water where you dream.

Forgive me that I have no gentleness
To be at home with you, nor business
To know you thoroughly, and only you.
With nothing done and nothing much to do
I wait to take you coldly by the hand,
Shaken with love I cannot understand.

A LEAF BLOWN UPSTREAM

Against the stream's cruel flow
A leaf is blown
Back towards the pool—
In this
The wind's wish
Being stronger than the stream's,
And the leaf's lack
Such
It will quite obey
The lie of its luck, this way or that,
Being lost
From any tall tree rooted in the land.

And will you catch
The rebel leaf
Before it is drowned or combed
To formal trash
In the too shallow bed?
Take it and hold it in your thrifty hand
To press to your cheek and use
As a sentimental mark
Between the pages
Of your unread book?
That one day, reading this,
You almost may remember
How I came to you
Much against your will,
From a tree we could not name?

NOT LOOKING

You notice I never look at you when I speak?
Perhaps you have seen in this something crooked—
A fear of meeting your eyes? You would be right
So to think, for my shame of your knowing is such
I'm frightened of your gaze clean through me
Proving my meaning little to you. Yet it is not just this.

I have a way of not looking, as you see,
Which is also part of a way of seeing.
If I do not return the long stare you offer
To search me with, and you might wish I'd learn,
It is because your presence is too sharp,
Your eyes too dear for my eyes, being poor.

I was never exactly frank, you know.
Besides, it's suitable to talk to smoky air
Knowing you near at hand, inhabiting
The corner of my eye, and half my heart.
If I looked straight at you I might say much;
Might even speak of love, which would not do.

ROPES

Watching the old man and the young man
Take ropes from round about the belly
Of the hay-waggon, you said,
'See how the old man coils and curls his rope
And brings it straight to hand,
While the young man leaves his ungathered.'
I knew that you looked down on what I'd wasted
But had not care enough to take it up
And make a neatness of it for your sake.

A PROPER PLACE

Outside my window
Two tall witch-elms
Toss their inspired
Green heads in the sun
And lean together
Whispering.

Trees make the world
A proper place.

A SMALL MERCY

Down in the wood the boys walk wild
Hunting for badger and fox;
Afraid of the dark, fulfilling its curse,
They kill what the moon loves.
Poet, be grateful they do not run
Nor hammer yet at your door,
To drive your pen through your open eye
And follow the night to its source.

ECHO

Standing outside the evening
I clap my hands together
To make the green woods answer
And the low hill send back meaning.

NARCISSUS

There sits the boy Narcissus, or some such,
  Kissing his outcast face, and crying for it.
Not that he need enjoy himself too much!—
  We know he is in love, and dying for it.

THE DICTIONARY COMES

Perhaps he ate the dictionary
Not for love or money
But because he was hungry?

Perhaps he drank blood
Not because he dreamed of Emily Brontë
Drinking his blood (which he did)
But because he was thirsty?

And now he is no longer
Lean with a young man's hunger,
Now all wild words are bloody
And blood and bone lack language,
What should he do—
Drink verbs in Africa with Rimbaud?
Make dirt his daily bread?
Or say, *This hunger and this thirst*
Were for myself, and brought no food for truth.

And even if he should say so
Might not in dream the dictionary come
To eat him whole?
The dictionary comes.
And blood completes his self-insulting flesh.

ROUGH OLD JOKER

He can cut straight down oak, to shape it well,
Just the right point, to make each piece a stake
For a white fence to keep black cattle out;
Yet with each blow he gasps as if the blade
Bit through his bone, and he the rough old joker
Who needed shaping, straightening, made sharp
To drive, or be down-driven, in the earth.
And is there tree-love in the way his hands
Chase down hewn sides, stripping the spills clean off,
Holding the finished stake up to the sun?
Or hate, perhaps, of knowing how this stood
As he has not, long in a growing wood?
In love or out, he knows his work will stand
After he has a longer stake in land.

CROWSON

He died at the proper time, on Christmas Day
As we sat down to dinner—an old man
With no friends and no vices, blindly mean
With the kind of love that goes with being clean,
His chief possessions a sour bar of soap,
A flannel which reeked of him, and a steel comb
He used to keep his dry grey hair in order
Over the face as hard and proud as a doorknob;
A sick old man, but acting out his illness,
A broken man, but whole and straight in cunning,
A man whom no one loved or liked or pitied,
Whom we had wished would die, for the work's sake.
And yet, I think, I did not wish him harm.

Well he was dead at last, on Christmas Day,
And spoiled our dinner. 'Just like him,' said Twitch,
'To go and die now, after seven months
Of not quite dying. Just like him to save
His death for the wrong time, when no one's ready.
Who wants to lay out a corpse on Christmas Day?
It would serve him right if we left him, eh?'
And I agreed (although I was dismayed
Not to feel much beyond an amateur's
Distaste for death), nodding in a paper crown,
Grinning at brother Twitch across a table
Set out with crackers, beer, cheap cigarettes.

Dinner completed and our bellies full,
Half-cut we went to Crowson's room.
He lay, the oxygen mask ridiculously sucked
Into his blue mouth, fish-eyes mocking us.
Beside the neat bed, on the locker,
His watch ticked fussily; his corpse

Scarcely disturbed the counterpane's perfection,
So thin he had become in these last days.
Twitch belched. 'We'd better get him over with.'

And then Twitch bullied
That sticky carcass, punched it here and there
About the bed, about the usual business:
A bag of bones shoved rudely in death's costume.
He mocked the stale flesh, fey in this last gesture—
'A Christmas present, darling'—tying a bow
On the penis, where a knot would have done,
Flirting with the shroud
As if it were the dress of some gay girl,
Taking revenge for all the dead one's age
And ugliness, knowing he would come
To this too soon—and, most of all,
For spoiling our Christmas dinner.

This is no elegy, for I did not love you,
Crowson, old man smelling of soap and tuberculosis;
Surely, for all my wrong, I did not love you
As queer Twitch did, who used you then so cruelly.
And yet, I think, I did not wish you harm.
Am I to blame for what he did to you?
The question in its asking answers 'Yes':
For where did Twitch begin and such fear end
As made me cold, incapable of tears
Or useful rage till this? and in these words
Which cannot warm you now, nor yet avenge
The insult you did not feel in my name,
The bullying no buffet could atone,
Nor prayer nor haunting expiate.

It was my faint white heart which hit you there.
It was my greed of self deflowered you
And bruised you in your death, which you thought perfect.

To ask forgiveness were another insult—
I will ask nothing but that you forget
You ever knew me, as I would forget
The big day I was born, keeping in mind
The day you died. I am forgetting now
In hope I will remember you more clearly
And in your memory wish no harm more dearly.

AN ANSWER FOR THE OWL

The night's anonymous, yet if the owl
Cries *Who? Who? Who?* while wind weeps in the hair
Of the long firs, then neither is forsaken:
Owl asks the wind, the wind will answer *You.*
Inside the house, where love has proper names,
I ask no questions in the name of love
When I cry *Who?* and try to make you weep.
An answer for the owl is all I want.

NOVEMBER SUN

The sun so low
In the sky today
A squirrel leaps over it
Going to his drey.

FISHING

At thirteen he went fishing for stars.
Either for lack of hooks or love of the strict twine
Which could be taught to shiver in the hand
He fished for them, saying he fished for crabs.

No bait gets glory. He used mussels.
After school he had searched the hard
And taken plenty when the tide was out;
Now each agape, its matter manifest,
His greed made fast with a half-Gordian knot
In a new context, and sent back to the dark
About its tacit business. He felt sure
Some star that lurked or smouldered in the net
Of stars below the surface could be caught.

Crab after crab came up, acknowledging
His wasteful magic and his innocence,
But still no star rose clinging to a shell.
Once, twice, he thought he had one, but
Only an unlucky starfish floundered, half-wound
In the sea-stained twine, mocking star-need.
Sick of ambition, tired of self-deceit,
He lost his sleight of hand, let all his gear
Ride with the tide, and sat and watched the moon.

Later he learned how not to fish too much—
Or, rather, how to fish for more than stars
With less than mussels or a singing line.
He fished for nothing. And he caught the sea.

IV

(1970–1976)

[illegible]
Walks beautifully down the long corridor
Of the drowned house [illegible]
At the turn of the century. [illegible] probably
It is without doubt October. [illegible]
[illegible] through high windows. The cranky portraits
Are thirteen [illegible] walking
On the thick [illegible] Henry James
It is [illegible] like the face of a [illegible]
[illegible]
[illegible]
[illegible]
[illegible]
[illegible]
[illegible]
Is complicated. [illegible]
Which [illegible] from [illegible]
Listen and you will hear the [illegible]
Our author has [illegible]
Above the words [illegible]
[illegible]
To simplify [illegible]
[illegible]
[illegible]
[illegible]
[illegible]
[illegible]
[illegible]
Henry James [illegible]
James goes beautifully [illegible]
a hand, [illegible]
The long [illegible]

HENRY JAMES

Henry James, top hat in hand, important, boring,
Walks beautifully down the long corridor
Of the drowned house just off Dungeness
At the turn of the century. It is 3 p.m. probably.
It is without doubt October. The sun decants
Burgundy through high windows. The family portraits
Are thirteen versions of the one face, walking
On the thick trembling stalk of Henry James.
It is a face which looks like the face of a goldfish
Fed full of breadcrumbs and philosophy, superbly
Reconciled to its bowl. The difference
Between Henry James and a goldfish, however,
Is that Henry James has nostrils. Those nostrils observe
An exquisite scent of evil from the library.
Henry James goes beautifully on his way. His step
Is complicated. (He nurses an obscure hurt. It is this
Which kept him from active service in the sex war.)
Listen and you will hear the trickle of his digestive juices—
Our author has lunched, as usual, well—
Above the sweetly unpleasant hum of his imagination.
His shoes make no squeak and he deposits no shadow
To simplify the carpet. Henry James
Turns a corner. Henry
James meets Henry
James. Top hat, etcetera. Henry James
Stops. Henry James stares. Henry James
Lifts a moral finger. 'You again!'
He sighs. 'How can you be so obvious?'
Henry James blushes and Henry James flees and Henry
James goes beautifully on his way, top hat
In hand, important, boring, he walks down
The long life-sentence of his own great prose.

THE LONG-AGO BOY

Sometimes I meet the boy I was.
He's the colour of lightning.
He leads me along stoat tracks,
Smudged with bright blood, in the snow.
He juggles with snowballs.

That boy lolls also in a hollow oak
Out of the sleet, and counts dead leaves
Like winnings. Up to his chin he is
In rusty guineas. He'll sniff
The pinesmoke in the candlelight
And the air on the green hill
Glorified with snow.

This boy has been busy tasting the frost
Spun like candy floss about
The spokes of a buckled bike.
Already he's sucked the icicles
That bristle from the eaves, and licked
The tongues sticking out of milkbottles.

The boy's ribs are bruised
By the bullying northpaw wind.
When he weeps, it's hailstones.
When he laughs, the loch gets gooseflesh.
The sun is bleeding to death
In a puddle of slush.
O long-ago boy, let's spit at it.
Tonight we'll claw all the stars down
That dangle from Orion's stupid belt.

TRAVELLING TO MY SECOND MARRIAGE ON THE DAY OF THE FIRST MOONSHOT

We got into the carriage. It was hot.
An old woman sat there, her white hair
Stained at the temples as if by smoke.
Beside her the old man, her husband,
Talking of salmon, grayling, sea-trout, pike,
Their ruined waters.

A windscreen wiper on another engine
Flickered like an irritable, a mad eyelid.
The woman's mouth fell open. She complained.
Her husband said: 'I'd like
A one-way ticket to the moon.
Wouldn't mind that.'

'What for?' 'Plant roses.' '*Roses?*' 'Roses,
Yes. I'd be the first rose-grower on the moon.
Mozart, I'd call my rose. That's it.
A name for a new rose: Mozart.
That's what I'd call the first rose on the moon,
If I got there to grow it.'

Ten nine eight seven six five four three two one.
The old woman, remember her, and the old man:
Her black shoes tapping; his gold watch as he counted.
They'd been to a funeral. We were going to a wedding.
When the train started the wheels sang *Figaro*
And there was a smell of roses.

HONG KONG STORY

I

Robespierre is coming to the conclusion
The late Mr Sing Sing is turning into an agnostic.
The back of the Chinaman's skull is a cinema
Where slatternly skirts trail in the mud
While he waits out of sight for an ankle to show.
A lock of glossy black hair hangs over his face,
Ink on ochre, like a magpie's wing. He weeps too much.
He confesses to so many crimes that the Police Commissioner
Is amused, then embarrassed, finally quite jealous.

II

Mr Sing Sing is a grotesque even by Hong Kong standards.
On the day of the murder he can't do his own hair.
The comb snaps. He trips over the encyclopedia
That serves him for a carpet. He lands on his head
By the door. It is not really a door. It is more
Of a ladder. He goes down it now for a lager.
Once in the saloon bar he delivers a rapid oration.
All he wants is employment as an artilleryman.
He picks up a sashweight. His hand is podgy.

III

Mr Sing Sing chants and the others join in.
He is inventing incidents in crusades.
He talks loudly, more and more sober. Some day
He'll cut it off. Yes he will.
He's killed all his prisoners.
(They seated themselves round the table in the death room.)
The republic is an elected nonsense,
Ignorance multiplied by rice.
A scarlet carriage means a violent death.

IV

General Romoza considers his maps. Roads, red roads,
Leading nowhere. There is a fire on the ground.
He runs from the sea to the hole and back again.
He elects to take the coast road. That makes sense.
There is no sky, only a murky collection
Of curt clouds. His skill returns. He clenches
His eyes. The stars are no more than a bouquet of ashes
In his sight. The small stones sing in the sand.
The moon of course is repeating herself on the night.

V

General Romoza arrives at the noble mansion.
Italian Gothic, it boasts a porte cochère,
A pinnacled tower, bold gables, embattled bays.
It is approached by a long dull drive
Under a snobbish avenue of beech trees.
Its innocence is preserved by a stone lodge
With an archway entrance also. Chinese lanterns
Swing with deliberation from mast and balcony.
The General brings the column to a halt.

VI

War, declares Robespierre, is not what we came for.
See a little lonesome stray snowflake come down
Through the air, he adds, it falls and melts and is no more.
Now see others come along in that soft gossiping way together,
And as they drivel on you can guess they've evidently
Got something on their minds. O yes, says Robespierre,
What they're thinking of is the rest of the bloody regiment
Massing up there in the clouds for an organized attack
That will make a drift thirty feet deep and stop our tanks.

VII

Robespierre's men shift their feet in a vallum of leaves.
They have heard all this before and never been impressed by it.
Robespierre approaches the Italian Gothic door.
Robespierre sits staring at the bedraggled skeleton.
(It is an inch or two shorter than his doubts.)
Robespierre's spirits rise. A pistol—certainly,
That appeals to the imagination. Robespierre strips.
He is on his way to becoming a logical sheep.
His body will be trapped in a wee black book.

VIII

Mr Sing Sing, flanked by guards, follows the Police
Commissioner
Into the dusk of the church. The organ sounds.
(It is that sprightly 9/16 canon in the 8ve
Used for light relief in *Die Kunst der Fuge*.)
Mr Sing Sing tears at his magpie hair.
The worst of the General's men are sprawled on the flagstones,
Polishing their rifles. Robespierre pirouettes.
He salutes briefly. Are you aware, says the Chinaman,
That your stomach acids could burn a hole in the carpet?

IX

Mr Sing Sing's togs are even more ostentatious
Than his criminal convictions. He wears a hussar's jacket—
High-buttoned, bottle-green, with appalling
Epaulettes—a pair of white cotton trousers
And brown riding boots of soft Hungarian leather.
The flickering of a thousand candles illumines
The Croix de Guerre unjustly on his chest.
Robespierre has sausage curls and employs a professional
To pick flowers for his wife. You're a long time dead, he
explains.

x

Sometimes I think I would like to live in Hong Kong
With Robespierre and General Romoza and Mr Sing Sing
On that island of sweet lagoons and thieves and yams
Floating off the south-west coast of China
Opposite the province of Kwang-tung, in the Si-kiang estuary.
They say its hills are serpentine, its animals few—
Comprising a land tortoise, the armadillo, a species of boa.
The public works suffer from the ravages of white ants.
It would be nice to sit there and eat pumpkin.

MY UNCLE

My uncle's hands were the colour of tobacco.
He sat and he listened to the river rattle.
He dreamt of logic.

My uncle's eyes were the colour of cider.
He sat and he listened to the rain coming on.
He dreamt of Dunkirk.

My uncle's hair was the colour of Bibles.
He sat and he listened to the Tilley lamp's hiss.
He dreamt of luck.

My uncle's face was the colour of allotments.
He sat and he listened to the tick of the clock.
He dreamt of forgiveness.

Now my uncle is dead and his bones are in the ground
And I sit and I listen to the river rattle
And I sit and I listen to the rain coming on
And the Tilley lamp's hiss and the tick of the clock
And my aunt making cakes in the kitchen.

TO A DICTIONARY MAKER

Sir, I believe in language too. Used well,
It puts our thoughts and feelings to a test
Whereby more than ourselves may be expressed;
It has a truth which we can learn to tell.
Help me to ring the changes on this bell—
I mean, the English tongue, the Saxon-blessed
And Latin-cursed linguistic of the best
Voices to modify a fear of hell.

What do I mean by hell? Sir, I mean fire.
I mean unmeaning and eternal flame
Defining nothing but our separation.
I mean what you meant when, a truthful liar,
Down on your knees you hallowed the one name
That stands between a man and such damnation.

INTERVIEW

What's it like, though, being you?
The old dog growls and bristles. This is his favourite question.
Answers win prizes. Nothing interests him more.
Inspired by the pursuit of his own tail
He has written his poems to find out what he smells like,
And now here's another dog, a dog-fancying thoroughbred,
Just down from Oxford, trained to the minute,
On heat and eager to do some of his sniffing
For him, and to declare the crap remarkable.
Woof woof, the old dog says, *bow wow.*
I'll show you where I buried my gift!

AGNUS DEI

On the shore
At the bend of the rock
A shrine:
Three ram skulls on a wall of pebbles.

A wall assembled by human hands,
Not looking natural in this place.
Altars never do.

The skulls all facing out to sea.
To the left, burnt
Into the rock, a capital letter A.
To the right, higher up, looking
Away, another (smaller) skull: a lamb's maybe.
Below, beyond the wall, a hollow
Where black ashes blow,
Stirred by the wind off the sea,
The rain, the grey haar.
To the right, down behind
A bush of thorns
On a narrow ridge
A small rectangular piece of marble,
Wafer-thin, depicting
A ewe with her lambs.

Below, a nail driven into the rock
And the nail holding
A scalp of seaweed,
And the seaweed brown and long
Like the hair of a young girl, a widow.

Above, the low cliff leaning,
The heather growing.
Great knots of roots hanging loose like severed nerves.
The rain grey and the sky falling through the thorns.

All three skulls having seaweed strips laid over them
Like hair, like a young girl's hair,
Like widowing.

READING ROBERT SOUTHEY TO MY DAUGHTER

Mr Robert Southey had the makings of a haberdasher
With a candy-striped shop in Bristol or Bath,
A secondhand carriage and a bow-legged mistress
With Jacobin leanings; but ambition and his aunt
Drove him to verse—
For which grand vice
He had no gift, only
A self-consuming facility.

Mr Robert Southey had the honour
Of wearing the Coleridges as his albatross.
Bad Lord Byron made his name rhyme with mouthy
And dignified him with fire also
In his Vision of Judgment.

At worst Southey R was a creepy crawly turncoat
Using little epics as tickets of admission
To the lower reaches of what he thought Society.
At best this esquire was a man who was better
Than anything he wrote. Coleridge said
His library was his wife.

O sweet O prolific O mediocre R
O ramblingly gallant and unimportant S
I remember how after the penultimate breakdown
Worn out with hacking you trotted up and down
Just stroking the spines
Of your seventeen thousand leather-bound concubines.

Mr Southey, man of letters, you worthy laureate
With such a thirst for righteous justice,
You once saw Shelley plain

And didn't care for it.
'What a dreadful thought of his wife's fate,'
You said, sir, 'what a dreadful thought
Must have come upon him when he saw himself
About to perish by water!'
Mahomet was no better.

O Robert O Southey if poor Percy Shelley
Screamed like a peacock, you clucked like a hen.
You had a kind heart but you geared it to royalties
And pensioned it off when the best time came.
Yet tonight, Robert Southey, I thank you by name
For the measure of a story you took and made better:
Not too fast, not too slow, not too hot, not too cold,
Not too hard, not too soft, not too long, not too short,
But just right for my Goldilocks—
Too young to say thank you
Herself, but who loves you
For loving just-rightness;
Bob of the Bears,
Our Southey friend.

IN MORE'S HOTEL

(for Aileen)

Wasn't it just that
We touched for the first time
The mother string
The pearls are threaded on?

Or was it especially
A key, a Bible—
A litany of chance
Which found again
Would spell us close
As we were then
In More's hotel,
Learning our alphabet?

Last night it was cloud
Against the pane, twice
You dreamt it.
This morning I turn on a tap and water
Is water alone, relating
To keys and Bibles
By a cordial difference,
Not very likely, but all the same
Married and holding together well.

ALL HALLOWS

Once as a child I saw the willows
Across the river at All Hallows,
Each one distinct although six miles away.
What brought them close and brings them now again
Sharp to the mind's eye like an icon of it?
An orthodox theology of tears.

A FORMER HOUSE

We had no mirrors in that house because
There were no faces there for mirroring.
We were the last of an incestuous line
Who raised the dead by looking at each other
In table tops and spoons, a family
In love with its own ghosts and origins,
Homeless at home with nowhere just next door.

IN MEMORIAM
JOHN COWPER POWYS
1872–1963

Knowing the horror of the house
More intimately than its mere ghosts,
You practised to unstitch
The mirror from its silver
And write down your name without wondering who.
O Prospero, no elegy for you.
You have been sent to Naples, that is all,
And this bare island is the barer for it.

FIVE DREAMS

I

I dreamt a dream, what can it mean?
I dreamt I went over a rainbow bridge.
I fell. I broke my neck.

II

I dreamt a dream, what can it mean?
I dreamt I wore a crown, a purple cloak,
Got stained with blood, or mud.

III

I dreamt a dream, what can it mean?
I dreamt I wandered in green fields
Where many sheep were grazing.

IV

I dreamt a dream, what can it mean?
I dreamt I went to a great theatre
Where all I saw was all I could remember.

V

I dreamt a dream. I know what it means.
I dreamt I threw a swallow in the sea,
And from the blood and foam a queen was born.

SHADOW ON A HILL

From where I stand on this bare hill
My shadow falls down land not mine
Like a long stranger, whose story
It has become to wait, unasked,
For an end of moon.

Broken shadow,
More miscellaneous to me now
Than when you went with roundhead swing
From I to I through a kingdom of selves
On nights before the moon was at the full:
You have grown cold in company you keep;
You have left nowhere for a barrener home.

ONE OR TWO SWALLOWS

One or two swallows, eager to be gone,
Over their heads passed where they sat upon
A tall hay-waggon riding from the sun.

He said, 'In autumn soon these flocks of birds
Will pluck the sky of music. Such cold chords
Send shivers down the spine. You mark my words.'

She marked his words and found it time to stop.
She was a poet so she shut him up.
'*They're just like tea leaves in an unwashed cup.*'

JOHN DONNE AND THE CANDLE

Do you remember a summer night
The sky deckle-edged with clouds
When you lay reading John Donne by a candle
On shadow-explicated pages?

I held a glass of water to the flame
To show you what a caught star might be like.
When I huffed out that little glory
There was a smell of mandrake.

PROLOGUE TO A MASK OF THE SEVEN DEADLY SINS

I am said to be made in the image of a mystery
Which may never be effaced however marred.
The likeness of God lies in the correspondence of the will.
Adam ate of the tree of the knowledge of good and evil.

It is not known whether that fruit was sweet or bitter,
Nor if without it the mind would have had a better taste.
You may suppose your own death to be a mistake
At least until you have been mistaken by it.

Meanwhile we will have sin to be going on with—
Which consists of so many little sips of the grave,
Original and actual: the sin of birth
And the seven sins of contradiction to eternal grace.

Glory be to the Father and to the Son and to the Holy Ghost.
We can't change human nature but God may
By means of a specific antidote
Which is called Christ and tastes like bread and wine.

BETWEEN

Ideas being only
Forms that are separate
Shadows of things,

Angels seeming harder,
The dream concurring
In its own act,

Somewhere between
Idea and *angel*
We make our way,

Half dream, half shadow,
Angelic intellectual
Ghosts who can bleed.

SIX SONGS

I

Must be listening
To your still aspect;
  Might be love.

Finding it difficult,
Couldn't be sure of
  You wholly other.

To your right hand
The water shapes
  The sun dances.

Nothing else says this.

II

You are clear metaphors:
The wind teaching
Itself
To read itself.
You are clear metaphors:
Light breaking
As soon as you offer it
Your straight shy look.

III

Sat down again
At the great feast of language,
Tasted those funeral meats.
Once this would do
To sweeten disfavour,
Blunt the heart's appetite.
Not any more.

IV

Afternoons of smoke pearl
Dissolved in the wine of the dark.
Your dress buttoned with stars.
Upriver the bright
Inheritable memories leap.
Your eyes as grey as lochs
Asking the tree what it is doing.

V

The hills of what you've done
Seem far too far away;
    Can't reach their care.

The moon's just a shadow of pearl,
Another vehement heart
    Repeating *Never go back*.

Nothing to see the sky with
But the sun saying over and over
    Too late now.

VI

This is for always:
Warm bread, cool water.
Despite the *nunc dimittis* of the rain
And the too long innocence of loaves
This I still wish you
Now and for ever:
Warm bread, cool water,
Flesh and blood miracles.

DIVISIONS ON A GROUND

I love you
Is like the sun's description
Of a field of green wheat.

I love you
Is like the wind's shadow
Tearing at the wound
Which joins it to the wind.

I love you
Is like the Blessed Virgin Mary
Falling at 32 feet per sec per sec.

A VOW TO DARKNESS

Darkness, I vow to you only that you are dark.
I have seen them blistering your eyelids with their white wafer
Who curse you, thinking they bless themselves.

As for me I knew you mostly in a bathroom
Where devils at their solipsist devotions
Strangled each other with soapy fingers, boasting
There is such company in hell!

V

(1977–1995)

THE WHITE FAWN

My weird's a fallow fawn, wild in the forest.
From Avalon she came, the bright foam skipping;
I know her presence by a scent of apples.

All summer long to catch her many Robins
In common green chased fleetly after moonbeams.
They dine on dreams who follow in her hoof-prints.

White is her coat and sallow her complexion;
No horns spring from that head so gently dipping.
I saw her once, and can adore no other.

Now, with midwinter come, and all fools parted,
Fulfilled of love I run, unfellowed, longing,
If only to touch snow her rut has rusted.

EURYNOME

Forgive me, Lord, who do not beg your pardon
Because I serve the lady of the garden,
Our mother Eve, who coupled once in Eden
Under the tree of life with father Adam.
She is Eurynome, the moon, my madam,
And there is none as wise or true or fair
In the wide earth, nor in the upper air.

EURYNOME AGAIN

So what if Orpheus' singing head
Dispraised Beatrice as it bled?
And Dante coming back from hell
Recalled Eurydice as well?
She who is queen of earth and air
Is richly named as she is rare.

THE SEWAGE PIPE POOL

I'd walk out on this sewage pipe to see
The quick, rich, swarming secrets of the pool.
Fat shrimps like garnets glowed in it, red crabs
Clawed sideways through its slime, once a pipe-fish
Got stuck, snout-up, half-baked in gummy scum—
And there was always bladder-wrack to pop,
A cluster of black grapes from the sea-bed.
I'd stir the lot with my stick. I was ten,
A good boy, not unhappy to be there.
Girls making cheeses with their petticoats
Also beguiled me, but the pool was best
Because its mysteries were mine to know
And my stick altered it and made them plain
Or readable at least, each barnacle
And rag-worm, goby and smudged jelly-fish
Part of a plot I spun, though not my own.

RIPOSTE

Above all other nights that night be blessed
On which my grandam rose from her sweet rest
Woke by a nightingale whose passionate song
Rang in the moonlight, Keatsian and long.
My grandmother threw open wide her door
And listened for a minute, not much more;
Then, when sufficient nightingale she'd heard,
Cried out: *Right! Just you bugger off, you bird!*

CHILDHOOD INCIDENT

One summer day at noon in our family kitchen
In my twelfth year I watched my mother cooking
The Collected Poems of Elizabeth Barrett Browning.

This was, I must admit it, a dirty book.
I had picked it out from an even dirtier junk-stall
Down in the market, near the church that used the incense.

Mrs Browning, as I remember, cost me sixpence—
Which was all my pocket money for a week—
But I forked out for her gladly on account of her famous love.

Alas as I took the book from the Pakistani stall-keeper,
Wiping the dirt of the years from it with my shirt sleeve,
This funeral came out of the church that used the incense . . .

Back home, my mother saw red at the sight of Mrs Browning
And when, in my stammering, I blurted out about the Pakistani
And then the purple coffin—well, it was just too much!

My mother took Elizabeth Barrett Browning in a pair of fire-tongs
And deposited her in the oven, turning the gas up high,
Remarking that this was the way to kill all known germs.

I feared then that what I would see would be the burning
Of Elizabeth Barrett Browning in our family kitchen;
But, praise to God, my mother knew her regulos.

I remember the venial smell of the baking
Of Elizabeth Barrett Browning in our family kitchen.
I can still see those pages that curled and cracked,

And the limp green leather cover that peeled away like lichen
From the body of the book, and the edges turning gold,
And the hot glue's hiss and bubble down the spine.

But most clearly I recall as if this was just yesterday
An odd but quite distinct and—yes—*poetic* scent
Which arose from the remains of Mrs Browning's Poems

When they came out baked and browned from my mother's oven
And lay steaming there on the table in the family kitchen.
It was, I swear to God, a whiff of incense.

GOING TO THE DOGS

Come Friday night my father's public vice
Was a greyhound track. He took me there twice.
Most of his life his own sad way he went,
So going to the dogs with me was different.

The electric hare, the eager racing hounds,
Tictacs in their white gloves, fistfuls of pounds—
The magic of that place and its event!
Oh, to me going to the dogs was different.

To choose a trap my poor Dad bruised his wits
Perusing form, and when that failed had fits
Of asking me my fancies. What this meant
For us made going to the dogs quite different.

Once the choice dog in the pre-race parade
Excreted what looked like bad marmalade.
'A sign,' my father said, 'from heaven sent!
You do know going to the dogs is different?'

He'd urge his favourite home with passionate cries.
The keenest still brings tears into my eyes:
'Come on, my son!' It was an accident
Which our dear going to the dogs made different.

I can't remember what my old man won;
God knows he lost much more in the long run.
His coat was shabby and his hat was bent,
But going to the dogs I found him different.

I do recall my father shook my hand
When our dog came in first. Now understand:
Some of us gamble when our hearts are spent.
My going to the dogs is not so different.

GARETH TO THE COURT

You ask why I drink in the gutter?
Not for reasons of love, nor self-hate.
Communion was never my poison;
All I want is my own liquor straight.
So, lady, I smell of the kitchen?
My adventures, brave sirs, mostly fail?
Kind friends, as you judge me, put this in:
I never got drunk on the grail.

TO A YOUNG POET

In a muck sweat you quarrel with them all—
The knights of the Round Table, squab and tall,
Sat down to meat.

There is a glamour on the hall: plates come
And go just as the diners wish, though some
Refuse to eat.

They say you have come here to spoil their feast
Whose real offence is innocence. At least
You took no seat.

See now the chessmen playing, square to square,
This game that has no purpose but despair
Or twin defeat.

You are a pawn in Camelot's strange chess,
Fit only to be sacrificed, or less,
Your play complete.

Let them say this of you when you are dead:
Although he lost his heart he kept his head
And did not cheat.

THE RAIN UPON THE ROOF

Listen. It is the rain upon the roof
Telling of who you loved but not enough,
Whispering of what is otherwise elsewhere.

It would be sweet on such a night to die,
Kissing another's lips, touching darkly,
Hearing the soft rain falling everywhere.

Save that the rain has voices which complain
You never loved enough, you were unkind,
You ran away, you left your heart nowhere.

Come back! Come back! The rain's regret may cease
But I will love you till my dying breath
And after, if there's after anywhere.

A CHARM AGAINST AMNESIA

No name you know reminds you now
Of who you are or why you go
Alone about your trouble in the snow.

Forgetting whom you would forget
You have forgotten more than that
And lost your mind's distinctive alphabet.

So if you trace your footprints back
To where you started, will that track
Supply the sure identity you lack?

The character of snow is white.
You cannot find your own delight
From marks made on it by your appetite.

Do not despair. There is one name
Which being known will make it plain
That you and wasted snow are not the same.

Call up the faces you recall
And see if from among them all
One hurts your heart and makes even cold tears fall.

That half-loved other is your fate—
Her name can turn you from hell's gate
And bring you home again before too late.

MOON FEVER

This is the scene to which I keep returning:
The moon is in her shroud, the sky is burning,
Under the streaming stars a heron stands
Like a sickle dipped in feathers; on the sands,
Beside where she is fishing, a silver eel
And speckled trout lie spread in a broken wheel.

I see the heron shiver from her trance
And rise upon the gleaming air askance.
I burn for her, yearning to follow after . . .
But am brought down to earth by your wise laughter
Who call this my moon fever, kissing me
On my hot eyes to stop the things I see.

IN PRAISE OF LIPSTICK

You lick your lipstick half the night
Yet have no need of this red paint
Whose lips are hot enough to burn a saint.

Sweet, such cosmetics serve you right
To put a new mouth on your face
So you can lie with me in my disgrace.

Lying apart, without delight
I praise your powder, salve, and scent,
While still suspicious what your kisses meant—

Lilies self-gilded look so innocent.

AGAINST PIGTAILS

It pleases you to plait your hair
Across your lovely head.
This pleasure, lady, I can't share—
Won't you come back to bed?
Drown me in your crowning glory!
Pigtails are another story.

A PLACE APART

We watch two candles melt together
In their last moments wondering whether
Hot wax and wicks are twisted of
Loathing or lust or even love.
Such burns illuminate the mind
But leave a tallow taste behind.
Grease-stained, smoke-fouled, the unquenched heart
Still keeps its shining place apart—
A glass that doubles each bright flame,
Making more light, though not the same
As this which smells of what it handles:
Our incandescence in the candles.

STORM

Hearing the crash of thunder out at sea
And the first dash of rain against the pane,
Watching the lightning's jagged tracery
And curtains that blow in then out again,
You lie awake in the crook of my arm
Complaining that you think I wish you harm
Even while crying that you love me still
And always have and always will
Who might as well love any other foe—
And do, for all I know.

THE CHRISTMAS WITNESS

I call midwinter back to hear you cry
O look at that, my dear! seeing some twig
By the frost's kiss or a soft touch of snow
Abruptly gifted with how bent a grace.
You were the Christmas witness all December
Once it came down to broken sticks and stalks
Surprised into a glory of themselves,
Making me heed and keep that festival
In which dead things achieve a kind of life
Just because frozen vapour blesses them.
Without such lessons in the art of solstice
I would see nothing much worth keeping here.

SONG OF THE HALF-CRACKED ECHO

Loving you might be
A way of walking
On snow on sand
On sand on snow
Between the breaking sky
And the broken sea.

Loving you might be
A way of dancing
On fire on frost
On frost on fire
Between the dying air
And the deadly earth.

Loving you might be
A way to remember
All I must forget
Forego forget
Between the breaking sky
And the dying air.

Loving you might be
A way to forget
All I must remember
Redeem remember
Between the broken sea
And the deadly earth.

MORE'S HOTEL REVISITED

(again for Aileen)

In More's hotel we touched for the first time
The mother strings from which all music comes.
Then everything in that translated place
Sang with the change—our room-key turned to gold
And burned in the lock; the bedside Bible
Fell open at the Song of Solomon;
The sheets were soft yet smelt like new-baked bread
And our hearts beat in a wild harmony.

That music we heard once in More's hotel
Was mortal, absolute, a simple theme
Which, being known, can never be forgot.
Instead of variations, I propose
We might go back to touch a second time
Erato's well-tuned strings, for a new song.

A BIT OF HONESTY

Love is the name they give out in Tasmania
To Traveller's Joy, which some call Virgin's Bower.
The thing itself is sweet, though not as mania
Would have us say, nor bitter in its flower
As those made mad by it sometimes protest.
It is as good a plant as all the rest—
No less, no more. In English parts, you see,
The name for this same thing is Honesty.
Here's honesty for you. Long may it live!
I'd give you love, if I had love to give.

WITHOUT PREJUDICE

To Spindle, Shears, and Rod,
Solicitors for God:
Dear madams, ref. the part
Enclosed herewith, my heart—
Please note this doesn't fit
The rest of the love kit
Supplied me by our father,
Your client, being rather
Too big to go with my head
Yet not big enough in bed.

CIRCE'S FAREWELL TO ULYSSES

Nothing can make you deaf, God knows, not moly
Nor bees-wax, certainly nothing holy
Can ever make you deaf to the half-pissed
Buzz of your own voice droning, atheist,
Busily bumbling on about your wanderings
And wounds and Troy and cooking-pots and kings
And bets and navigational aids and your sciatica
And how much things would cost back home in Ithaca.
You bum—here, take your ticket to hell's halls.
Tiresias could use your story. You talk balls.
As for me, sunshine, I've had more than enough
Of it and you, so goodbye to all that stuff,
And farewell, Ulysses! Ulysses to hell!
Sweet Circe wishes you safe home as well,
Requesting never again to hear, for choice,
Of your Life and Works, or your influence on James Joyce.

LATE VICTORIAN SONNET

Dead leaves his cloak, his only wand the swan
Drawing a silent circle on the lake
To conjure several old boots in its wake,
The Queen's still potent but disgraced magician,
Oscar the Wild—whose last amazing trick
Turned all the usual sweets of summer sick—
Having done time for this crime of not sawing
Women in half, bursts out of gaol he-hawing
Like the bad ass he is, unbuttoning his flies . . .
Trumpets arrest him! Oscar blinks his eyes.
A pearl-pale hand beckons from a closed carriage.
Veiled lady. A proposal. It is not marriage.
Oscar is honoured, though the act's obscene,
And buggers off to Paris with the Queen.

THE SISTERS

Quick snow is falling, melting as it falls;
She stands between the fireplace and the night
Watching each soft flake flower on the pane,
Half-listening to her sister playing scales—
Their old piano's keys that click and stick—
While in the grate coals crackle together.

These things are more real to you than the scene
You know on waking, but are not a dream:
Notes rising, falling, tired music talking
About the instrument on which it plays;
A firelit room, uncurtained; two sisters
Themselves more slow to vanish than the snow.

Oh, who are they? And where is this grey house?
You have seen one sister perhaps, though not
At a winter window all mothed over.
The details of the vision fall apart;
It was your need first drew them together
Into a storm of changes and desire.

Still, do not doubt that soon enough you'll stand
Between night and the sisters, in the porch
Of the old house, hearing that piano.
And when the music stops and the door opens
Who will you say you are, and why come hither
Out of a world where snow melts as it falls?

CATCHING LEAVES

The boy you were caught leaves that fell
From trees he could not name.
The man you are must try to tell
Rowan from ash, yet run as well
To catch each falling flame
And hope upon its fame.

THE CASTLE OF THE PERFECT ONES

You'll eat no honey in that bee-hive house
(They need no sweets who are themselves so pure)
But in your ears a buzz of holy hymns
Will sound all day, all night, immaculate,
Making the door vibrate on its cracked hinges.
What would you give to pass that door again
And see the stars from the shelving side of the hill!

The prick of perfection lengthens any note
By one exacting half . . . So will they stretch you,
Those moral musicians, to your highest pitch
And half a time beyond it. You will know
You are in royal purgatory all right,
A voice in the eternal choir that sings
From the dark tower at the back of the north wind.

Whether this is your home is not the question.
Once in the Castle of the Perfect Ones
Better to be a perfect one yourself
Than to go mad longing for imperfections.
It could be worse. At least you will be faultless
And have no need of honey, stars, or sex:
O pure O self-complete O perfect fool.

MEMORY

The Lady Memory disguised in moonlight
Walks the walled garden that I call my mind.
She is the mother of the other Muses;
If you approach her gently you may find
Her shadow is a nightingale, her dress
Some silken thought of long-spun tenderness.

Memory's face reminds me of her daughters
Who once were the delight of my despair.
I have forgotten much, but still remember
The way they sang their songs and combed their hair
On a green hillside where a grove of trees
Made music like a swarm of summer bees.

Peace to those beauties who have left me here
With my own words to eat, a bitter diet
Sweetened by drinking from the Pierian spring.
Good morning, Memory; it is your quiet
I must learn now, not so much reticence
As knowing little can improve on silence.

ON A LEAF USED AS A BOOK-MARK

A leaf, blown back towards the pool
Against the stream's unwavering flow,
Obeys the wind's soft-spoken wish
To have it so.

So once was I instruction's fool
Upon the surface of delight,
Compelled to contrariety
By day, by night.

You took me in your thrifty hand,
You plucked me from the burning brook;
You dried me out and cured me
In your good book.

Now no more flotsam, I'm the mark
Which tells you how much you have read.
I who was wind-blown and alive
Lie here, not dead.

TO THE OTHER

You haunt me whom I have not seen;
You taunt me with what might have been.
O why? Unknown one, I don't know,
But know it must be always so
Until we meet and, in our meeting, find
We are two strangers who are of one mind.

LULLABY

Running waters dark and deep
Stand beside you where I stood,
My daughter, as you rock to sleep
In the dabbling cradle-keep.
Queen Habundia give you ease
And our only lawful lord,
The wind, bid you a last good-
night, as the moving waters cease,
My daughter, as you are asleep.

THE DEVIL'S JIG

Submarines wrinkled the Nore like moles,
Earth-wet and auburn, when he was a boy.

It was not always so—the Thames in flood,
An eyelash with a thousand years to fall.

The day he ran as fast as the east wind
A wasp stung him on the eyelid.

No nightingale choked with tears amused him.
His metaphysics was a kind of fishes.

The fragile mazes of the estuary
Taught him the way to hell and poetry.

Writing a poem in a mirror he
Heard a blind fiddler in the alleyway,

And knew the devil's jig was more
Or less what he was writing for.

The moon's full and needs a shave.
He wished his bones could dream without his flesh.

POPPIES

Poppies who could not slip their dew
Into the dreaming of the stream
As a bright breath against identity
Were less than identifications
Or metaphors in memory made wilful:
Sneak-thieves of plausible self-wakefulness.

ENOUGH

Earth is enough for the earth-born.
You tell me that a unicorn
Rubs his white horn between your paps:
So you belong to heaven, perhaps.

A PRAYER*

If I am not in the grace of God
May God place me there;
And if I am in the grace of God
May God keep me there;
For I should be the saddest in all the world
If I knew I was not in the grace of God.

*Said in the form of Joan of Arc's answer to the question 'Do you know if you are in the grace of God?'

THE FROGS

I saw two frogs under a stone
Doing what we do when we are alone.

Belly to back in their foul pool
They did what we do darkly as a rule.

The male frog was a bunch-backed chap.
He clasped his froggy consort to his lap.

The female frog was small and plump.
She shook with lust and took him up her rump.

Their eyes were bright, their mouths agape;
It was a sweet unconscionable rape.

An age I watched them in their slime
Doing what I do now in my black rhyme.

Their frogging done, they had a piss.
Christ send me, quick, another night like this.

SAPPHO

A peacock loved her
But that was in Leucadia.
She can remember
Only his strutting,
His clumsy rutting,
The way he mocked her song with his smooth screams.

Madam, there are dreams
In which the peacock is no bird of prey.
Pity your fellow his poor pride. You may,
Since even in Leucadia
Some do not strut
But walk towards darkness with their bright eyes shut.

THE RAIN IN THE EAVES

The eaves drip rain. It is the eaves
I listen to now as I sit and write.
Some nights the moon comes up in glory
And I scent civet on my sleeves
Where her dress brushed me. But tonight
Just the rain in the eaves tells her story.

It is the saddest tale to tell
And the rain knows that, and tells it well,
Chapter by chapter, bit by bit,
Devil by devil, all of it
In the same drumming monotone—
A voice I could almost believe was my own.

But it is not my tale I write
As I sit up and listen half the night
To the rain in the eaves that mourns and grieves
And frets away at the rotting leaves
Which make it sound like the voice of the dead
Telling her story in my head.

If I could tell her tale I would
But for all I can tell it would do no good.
I tell you the sound of the rain in the eaves
Telling a story no one believes,
Telling a story without any art
I tell you the sound of the rain in my heart.

The eaves drip rain. It is the eaves
I listen to now as I sit and write.
Tomorrow the moon may rise in glory
And there might be civet on my sleeves
Where her dress touched me. But tonight
Let the rain in the eaves tell her story.

ADMONITION ON A RAINY AFTERNOON

Do not suppose your tender touch
Will make her love or even like you much.
There is no Lydian measure in your clutch.

To hold on now were less than sense.
Worse, it might match the long day's decadence.
Wet weather makes the fiddle-strings more tense.

Forego the rain, let go before
All is unstrung, or she may loathe you more
Than you deserve who'd make of her a whore.

Let go, let go, my heart, and take
Your pleasure elsewhere, for Erato's sake,
Whether it's love or music that you make.

HOSPITAL INCIDENT

The boy lies dying in the hospital
And his mother has brought him oranges:
They glow in the green glass bowl by his bed.
All afternoon he considers their shining skins
While the old men in the ward attempt to cheer him:
'Eat up your oranges, cocker, there's a good lad.'

The men's ward and the women's lie side by side.
On summer nights the women sit up in their beds
Brushing their hair, and calling across to the men.
Those oranges burn in the bowl on the boy's locker.
He is sixteen years old. He will never be older.
He stares at that ripe fruit which he will not eat.

Night comes. The lights are lit in both the wards.
The summer air is quick with the noise of insects.
The women call to the men across the grass.
The boy jerks to his feet. He asks the ward orderly
To tie the tape tight which holds his pyjama trousers.
The orderly ties it, and tries to return him to bed.

The boy picks an orange and holds it out, grinning.
'Just once,' he says quietly. 'Like Fred Trueman.'
He is polishing the orange against his groin.
His eyes are bright with tears and angry longing
For what he will never do or know or have.
The orderly shrugs and smiles. He turns his back.

The boy takes three deep breaths of oxygen
Then lurches towards the door on the verandah—
His arm swings over and he bowls full-toss
Into the dark. 'Ladies!' he shouts. 'How's that?'
The orange shatters the square of light opposite,
Smashing the great main window of the women's ward.

The old men don't like this. They ring their bells.
Nurses come running. In the women's ward
They ring bells too, and call out for their nurses.
The boy does not need nurses, nor these bells.
He lies face down in his blood. He is soon dead.
How's that, ladies? Just once. Pardon him.

WHEN ALL IS SAID AND DONE

I have not read
The answer to life is no
And the man who wrote it is dead.
I know his name was Ray or Wray something
But beyond that, nothing.

This is to say
I remembered him today.
I remembered I had not read
Wray so-and-so's autobiography
The answer to life is no
Having supposed it not my show,
Believing I did not need to read it
Or know anything else about it
Except its name.
So much for fame.

I met him once—
Wray who-what-ever, ah Wrey Gardiner, yes.
He pissed himself and spoke of tenderness.
I can't say that I blame him,
And now I'm glad to name him.
When all is said and done
He's not the only one.
If I am given gifts I do not want
I give them to my mother who gave me
The gift of life. And I have left my marks.
One night I might
Breathe on the glass myself and write
The answer to life is no.
Perhaps. It is not vital.
But it's a damned good title.

HARES DANCING

Once, once I stood
By a green wood
And watched hares in the snow.
Against the light
They reared upright
As they danced there to and fro.
And the sun stood still
On a silver hill
And the wind forgot to blow.

Those hares ran wild.
I was a child
And tears ran down my face
To see them dance
As in a trance
In that white and holy place.
And the dark night fell
But I knew quite well
I was in a state of grace.

Long, long ago
It was, I know,
And I have other cares.
I lie and weep
And cannot sleep
As pain at my heart's core tears.
I will close my eyes
And see no more lies
But dance with the dancing hares.